*Bibliographical Series*
*of Supplements to* 'British Book News'
*on Writers and Their Work*

GENERAL EDITOR
Geoffrey Bullough

TO.THE.ONLIE.BEGETTER.OF.
THESE.INSVING.SONNETS.
Mr.W.H. ALL.HAPPINESSE.
AND.THAT.ETERNITIE.
PROMISED.

BY.

OVR.EVER-LIVING.POET.

WISHETH.

THE.WELL-WISHING.
ADVENTVRER.IN.
SETTING.
FORTH.

T. T.

WILLIAM SHAKESPEARE

# THE POEMS

by

## F. T. PRINCE

PUBLISHED FOR
THE BRITISH COUNCIL
AND THE NATIONAL BOOK LEAGUE
BY LONGMANS, GREEN & CO

LONGMANS, GREEN AND CO LTD
48 Grosvenor Street, London, W.1

*Associated Companies, branches and
representives throughout the world*

*First published 1963
Reprinted with additions to bibliography 1968*
©F. T. Prince 1963

*Printed in Great Britain
F. Mildner & Sons, London, EC1*

# CONTENTS

¶WILLIAM SHAKESPEARE was born at Stratford-on-Avon, and was christened in the Parish Church on 26 April 1564. He died at Stratford on 23 April 1616, and at some date before 1623 a commemorative monument was erected at his place of burial, the Chancel of the Parish Church.

# SHAKESPEARE: THE POEMS

*Venus and Adonis* was published in 1593, *Lucrece* in 1594. *The Phoenix and Turtle* appeared in 1601, and the Sonnets (together with *A Lover's Complaint*) in 1609. All that we have of Shakespeare's non-dramatic poetry is printed within the twenty years when he was active as a dramatist, and there is no evidence that any of it was written before, say, 1592.

## I. *VENUS AND ADONIS*

Greene refers to Shakespeare in 1592 as an actor lately turned playwright, and rousing envy by his success. But in the summer of 1592 the London theatres were closed by an unusually violent outbreak of the plague; the closure continued throughout 1593. The players were hard-hit, and the young actor-dramatist probably sought to make up for his losses by writing and publishing two highly-coloured 'narrative' poems: besides what the booksellers might give him for them, he could expect a gift in money from some nobleman who was disposed to patronize poetry and the drama.

Both poems are dedicated to the Earl of Southampton, who was then a young man of twenty. The dedication of *Venus and Adonis* promises 'some graver labour', if the first offering is well-received (no doubt the words were written when it was already apparent that the players would remain unemployed for another season). *Lucrece* is the more serious work so foreshadowed; and the greater confidence and fervour of its dedication may reflect in part the fact that Southampton's response in hard cash had been quite as generous as the author had hoped.

Shakespeare, here as in the plays, 'for gain, not glory, wing'd his roving flight'. Both poems are designed to please. Both are a display of poetic beauty and wit; both have a strong erotic appeal. Of the two, the first is the more sensual, obviously spiced for the taste of courtiers and young men about town.

The Goddess of Love is in love. 'She's love, she loves, and yet she is not lov'd' (610); for she offers her full-blown, immortal beauty to a boyish, unripe, human lover. Still untouched by desire and self-centred, he neither needs nor understands her; indeed he resents and fears her, preferring his chastity, his freedom, his hunting, and the company of his hounds and horses. The action consists in Venus' wooing of the reluctant youth; his rejection and evasion of her; his death in hunting the boar; her grief, and the transformation of his body and blood to a flower, which will preserve his memory.

Shakespeare based his version of the myth on Ovid's, using elements from two other stories, those of Salmacis and Hermaphroditus and of Narcissus (*Metamorphoses* X, IV, III). The first instalment of *The Faerie Queene* had been printed in 1590; the Ovidian picture of the loves of Venus and Adonis and the adornments of the House of Busirane in Book III, and Acrasia's Bower of Bliss in Book II, lie behind *Venus and Adonis*; while there is a clear influence from Marlowe's *Hero and Leander*, as yet unpublished but circulating in manuscript.

Shakespeare was not concerned to invent a new form or style, but to do in his own way, and as brilliantly as possible, what other Elizabethans had tried already. He brings to the frivolous subject his personal sense of reality, and his unique energy. He writes as a countryman, and his classical landscape has the air and denizens of rural England. He writes also as a comic dramatist, seeing the pathos and absurdity of lovers at cross-purposes:

> He sees her coming, and begins to glow,
> Even as a dying coal revives with wind;
> And with his bonnet hides his angry brow,
> Looks on the dull earth with disturbed mind,
>     Taking no notice that she is so nigh,
>     For all askance he holds her in his eye.

O what a sight it was, wistly to view
How she came stealing to the wayward boy!
To note the fighting conflict of her hue,
How white and red each other did destroy!
   But now her cheek was pale, and by and by
   It flash'd forth fire, as lightning from the sky. (337-48)

Full gently now she takes him by the hand,
A lily prison'd in a gaol of snow,
Or ivory in an alablaster band:
So white a friend engirts so white a foe.
   This beauteous combat, wilful and unwilling,
   Show'd like two silver doves that sit a-billing. (361-6)

The young Shakespeare delights not only in the banquet offered to his imagination by perfect youth and beauty but in the clash of wills, the conflict between desire and its object, between mortal flesh and immortal, yet helpless, passion. The struggle is enhanced by being set in a spacious and lovely natural demesne, suggested in incidental details and digressions:

'Bid me discourse, I will enchant thine ear,
Or like a fairy trip upon the green,
Or like a nymph, with long dishevell'd hair,
Dance on the sands, and yet no footing seen.
   Love is a spirit all compact of fire,
   Not gross to sink, but light, and will aspire.

'Witness this primrose bank whereon I lie:
These forceless flowers like sturdy trees support me.
Two strengthless doves will draw me through the sky
From morn to night, even where I list to sport me.'
                             (145-54)

But lo from forth a copse that neighbours by,
A breeding jennet, lusty, young and proud,
Adonis' trampling courser doth espy,
And forth she rushes, snorts and neighs aloud:
   The strong-neck'd steed being tied unto a tree,
   Breaketh his rein, and to her straight goes he. (259-64)

Venus is quick to point the moral (385-408). The episode spreads into a full description of the perfections of the run-away steed, and his movements:

> Sometime he scuds far off, and there he stares;
> Anon he starts at stirring of a feather.
> To bid the wind a base he now prepares,
> And where he run or fly, they know not whether,
>   For through his mane and tail the high wind sings,
>   Fanning the hairs, who wave like feather'd wings.
>
> (301-6)

The elaborated episode or digression was a feature of the Alexandrian idylls, or little epics, from which Marlowe's and Shakespeare's poems are descended. In *Venus and Adonis* the episode of the mare and stallion and the description of the hunted hare (673-708) are strictly functional: they open out the landscape setting, and introduce a racy flavour of country life. While horse and mare are emblems of the cosmic sexual force which rules Venus herself, they also enable Shakespeare to surround his sultry theme with the freedom and freshness of the open air.

For Shakespeare human life is a moving, vivid spectacle, in which he delights to participate by contemplating and recreating it in poetry. In his intense enjoyment of beauty he seems at times to lose himself, but it is only for a moment; the next moment he is detached, and sees everything with new eyes. The mixture of sympathy and detachment comes out more and more in the treatment of Venus, from the point at which Adonis escapes from her at nightfall, and the comments on her 'woeful ditty', to the description of her half-hysterical anxieties as she follows the sound of the hunt:

> And as she runs, the bushes in the way,
> Some catch her by the neck, some kiss her face,
> Some twine about her thigh to make her stay;
> She wildly breaketh from their strict embrace,
>   Like a milch doe, whose swelling dugs to ache,
>   Hasting to feed her fawn, hid in some brake.      (871-6)

Above all, within the poet's delighted, absorbed vision of life, there lurks a sense of life's pain and danger. Hence Shakespeare's breadth of perception. He is able to enter into the emotional experience of both the eager goddess and the unmoved boy. Her persuasions to love are no more eloquent than his denunciation of lust:

> 'Torches are made to light, jewels to wear,
> Dainties to taste, fresh beauty for the use,
> Herbs for their smell, and sappy plants to bear:
> Things growing to themselves are growth's abuse.
>     Seeds spring from seeds, and beauty breedeth beauty;
>     Thou wast begot, to get it is thy duty.'   (163-8)

> 'What have you urg'd that I cannot reprove?
> The path is smooth that leadeth on to danger.
> I hate not love, but your device in love
> That lends embracements unto every stranger.
>     You do it for increase: O strange excuse,
>     When reason is the bawd to lust's abuse!

> 'Call it not love, for love to heaven is fled,
> Since sweating lust on earth usurp'd his name;
> Under whose simple semblance he hath fed
> Upon fresh beauty, blotting it with blame;
>     Which the hot tyrant stains and soon bereaves,
>     As caterpillars do the tender leaves.'   (787-98)

If anything, it is the rejection of lust that is poetically more powerful: it has more originality and force than the facile *carpe diem* of Venus. The opposition between love and lust may seem unimportant here, since the intent and spirit of the piece are so unmistakably sensuous. *Lucrece* does indeed bear witness to Shakespeare's involvement in the horrors of physical desire; but it is only by reading the Sonnets that we come to realize how important these emotional disharmonies were to be for Shakespeare.

## II. *THE RAPE OF LUCRECE*

*Lucrece* is a much longer poem than *Venus and Adonis;* written in a longer stanza, it also relates a more complex action, introducing more than the two chief characters. But its greater length is due even more to the greater elaboration of its style; the lightness of touch so well sustained in the earlier poem is here replaced by a tendency to labour the conceits (first apparent in lines 52-72); to moralize as fully as possible (for example, in lines 134-54); and to extract the last ounce of emotion from the heroine's sufferings.

On the whole, it appears that Shakespeare finds it more difficult to be serious than light-hearted; he makes a visible effort to sustain the tragic tone. In *Lucrece* he has put on the mask of tragedy, to produce a companion piece and contrast to the comedy of *Venus and Adonis;* and his notion of tragedy at this time is what we find in *Titus Andronicus* (which contains many verbal parallels to *Lucrece*), not in *Hamlet* or *Lear*. Crime and bloodshed, whether rape or murder, mutilation or suicide; the sufferings of the innocent, and a clash between violent evil and purest virtue: these are the ingredients of a form of tragedy associated with Seneca and classical mythology, which in Shakespeare's hands takes on a lurid vitality.

Yet in *Lucrece* his dramatic genius is working in a form which lacks the checks and supports of stage drama. Plunging into the narrative ('this pamphlet without beginning') with the impetuosity with which he launches a play and often carries through his first acts, he soon becomes entangled in comments and conceits, and is liable to let the soliloquies and speeches spread too far. He is struggling both with the abundance of his gifts and with the inherent lack of discipline in the showy, digressive type of pseudo-narrative he has undertaken.

In spite of these handicaps (if we can call exuberant genius a handicap), there are many passages where balance and efficiency are achieved, and the interest and emotion are maintained, not dissipated. Such, for example, is the description of Tarquin's rousing himself to steal through the sleeping house, and the expression of his guilty fears and resolutions (162-364). Even here we notice a passing tangle of conceits, when Shakespeare seeks to describe the ravisher's divided mind (281-99). Yet the same method can elsewhere succeed in creating authentic excitement and urgency, as in the passage in which he first gloats over his sleeping victim, then lays hands on her:

> As the grim lion fawneth o'er his prey,
> Sharp hunger by the conquest satisfied;
> So o'er this sleeping soul doth Tarquin stay,
> His rage of lust by gazing qualified,—
> Slak'd not suppress'd, for standing by her side
>   His eye which late this mutiny restrains,
>   Unto a greater uproar tempts his veins.

> And they like straggling slaves for pillage fighting,
> Obdurate vassals fell exploits effecting,
> In bloody death and ravishment delighting,
> Nor children's tears nor mothers' groans respecting,
> Swell in their pride, the onset still expecting.
>   Anon his beating heart, alarum striking,
>   Gives the hot charge, and bids them do their liking.

> His drumming heart cheers up his burning eye,
> His eye commends the leading to his hand;
> His hand, as proud of such a dignity,
> Smoking with pride, march'd on to make his stand
> On her bare breast, the heart of all her land;
>   Whose ranks of blue veins, as his hand did scale,
>   Left their round turrets destitute and pale.   (421-41)

*Lucrece* is full of brilliantly visualized moments of drama. Sometimes they are rapid and emblematic, when Lucrece in Tarquin's clutches,

> Like a white hind under the gripe's sharp claws,
> Pleads in a wilderness where are no laws,  (543-4)

or when she begins to tell Collatine what has happened:

> And now this pale swan in her wat'ry nest
> Begins the sad dirge of her certain ending. (1611-12)

Sometimes they describe concentrated character and action:

> He like a thievish dog creeps sadly thence,
> She like a wearied lamb lies panting there;
> He scowls, and hates himself for his offence,
> She desperate, with her nails her flesh doth tear.
> He faintly flies, sweating with guilty fear;
>   She stays, exclaiming on the direful night,
>   He runs, and chides his vanish'd loath'd delight.
>                                           (736-42)

The finest example of such skill in visual writing is the description of the paintings, or painted cloths, of the Siege and Fall of Troy, with which Shakespeare finally provides Lucrece with 'means to mourn some newer way' (1365):

> A thousand lamentable objects there,
> In scorn of nature, art gave lifeless life:
> Many a dry drop seem'd a weeping tear,
> Shed for the slaughter'd husband by the wife;
> The red blood reek'd to show the painter's strife,
>   And dying eyes gleam'd forth their ashy lights,
>   Like dying coals burnt out in tedious nights.  (1373-9)

The whole of this passage (as far as 1568) is carried through with speed and gusto, and forms one of the peaks of the poem. Shakespeare's picture-making is less pleasing when it shows a lingering delight in prettiness, as in the picture of Lucrece asleep (386-406) or the playing with the maid's tears of sympathy (1226-39).

Many passages in *Lucrece* anticipate dramatic effects or themes in plays written later: for example, in both *Macbeth* and *Cymbeline* night and crime are associated with Tarquin; and the story of Troy continued to appeal to Shakespeare's imagination.

In summing up *Lucrece* one is forced continually to qualify praise with reserve. It is a brilliant, uneasy, luxuriant work, and its greatest beauties can hardly compensate for its obvious faults. Some of these faults lie in exaggerated and superfluous detail: such a passage as 1107-48 cries out for excision. Yet the main fault is fundamental to Shakespeare's method, which may be stated briefly, as here applied: Lucrece is made to be the Chorus to her own tragedy. Thus there would be general agreement that the most magnificent writing in the poem occurs in the long central tirade, in which the heroine declaims against Night, Opportunity, Time, and finally Tarquin (764-1036). And within the surging violence of this great outcry, the finest passages are those in which her passion rises to universal themes, and Shakespeare sees the patterns of human experience and frailty as from a great distance:

> 'O opportunity, thy guilt is great! . . .

> 'Thou mak'st the vestal violate her oath;
> Thou blow'st the fire when temperance is thaw'd;
> Thou smother'st honesty, thou murder'st troth,
> Thou foul abettor, thou notorious bawd!
> Thou plantest scandal, and displacest laud:
>    Thou ravisher, thou traitor, thou false thief!
>    Thy honey turns to gall, thy joy to grief.

> 'Thy secret pleasure turns to open shame,
> Thy private feasting to a public fast,
> Thy smoothing titles to a ragged name,
> Thy sugar'd tongue to bitter wormwood taste;
> Thy violent vanities can never last.
>    How comes it then, vile opportunity,
>    Being so bad, such numbers seek for thee?

'When wilt thou be the humble suppliant's friend,
And bring him where his suit may be obtained?
When wilt thou sort an hour great strifes to end,
Or free that soul which wretchedness hath chained?
Give physic to the sick, ease to the pained?
   The poor, lame, blind, halt, creep, cry out for thee;
   But they ne'er meet with opportunity.'  (867-903)

When the theme becomes Time, we have the pulse of an
inspiration which we find in many of the Sonnets and the
plays:

'Time's glory is to calm contending kings,
To unmask falsehood and bring truth to light,
To stamp the seal of time in aged things,
To wake the morn and sentinel the night,
To wrong the wronger till he render right,
   To ruinate proud buildings with thy hours,
   And smear with dust their glittering golden tow'rs;

'To fill with worm-holes stately monuments,
To feed oblivion with decay of things,
To blot old books and alter their contents,
To pluck the quills from ancient ravens' wings,
To dry the old oak's sap and cherish springs,
   To spoil antiquities of hammer'd steel,
   And turn the giddy round of fortune's wheel; . . .

Why work'st thou mischief in thy pilgrimage,
Unless thou could'st return to make amends?
One poor retiring minute in an age
Would purchase thee a thousand thousand friends . . .'
                   (939-63)

Shakespeare is never more himself than when he can harness
such a metaphysical or moral topic to an individual passion.
Constance mourning for Arthur, Richard II lamenting his
folly and fall, express themselves in poetry recognizably
akin to this. Is the difference between its effectiveness and
the ineffectiveness of *Lucrece* merely a difference in proportion, or does it lie in the occult power of a dramatic frame-

work, which makes us accept the *articulateness* of the chief
characters? Perhaps most of Shakespeare's tragic characters
could be said to act as Chorus to their own tragedy; yet
when Lucrece does so, not even the magnificence of the
poetry Shakespeare gives her can disguise the incongruity.

The tirades against Time and Opportunity, like the
pictures of Troy, represent Shakespeare's attempt to give
the central theme a wider setting of human suffering, as he
does by means of the secondary plot in *Lear*. They corres-
pond to the digressions in *Venus and Adonis*. If they are less
successful, it may be because they are tied too closely to the
heroine's direct expression of her own suffering.

*Lucrece*, though a masterpiece of Renaissance rhetoric, is
undoubtedly flawed; but it provides invaluable evidence of
what Shakespeare could and could not do, at this stage, in
tragic poetry. Moreover, its handling of sexual desire, and
particularly of the torments of lust and guilt, tells us much
about Shakespeare's temperament and imagination, and may
help us to approach the Sonnets with more understanding.


## III.   SONNETS (i)

'Shakespeare's Sonnets' ('Never before Imprinted') were
published by Thomas Thorpe in 1609, in a Quarto volume
containing also 'A Louers complaint. By William Shakespeare'. No other edition appeared before Shakespeare died
in 1616, and all later editions derive from the Quarto. Two
sonnets (138 and 144 in 1609) had been printed in inferior
versions in *The Passionate Pilgrim* of 1599. The text of 1609
is less free from printer's errors than the Quartos of *Venus
and Adonis* and *Lucrece*, which were seen through the press
with some care, presumably by the author. But there is no
evidence that the book was pirated, or that Shakespeare did
not approve of its publication.

Francis Meres referred in 1598 to Shakespeare's 'sugred
Sonnets among his private friends'; but this does not tell us

how many then existed, or how far they went back in time. Yet it has been widely assumed that the Sonnets belong mainly to the 1590s, and nothing in them seems incompatible with either the state of Elizabethan poetry then, or Shakespeare's own style in the poems and plays attributed to those years. The feverish writing of love-sonnets was set off by the publication of Sidney's *Astrophel and Stella* in 1591; that volume also contained some sonnets by Samuel Daniel in what we call the Shakespearean form, which had been favoured by the poets of *Tottel's Miscellany* forty years earlier, but which Sidney had excluded from his sequence. Some of Daniel's sonnets of 1591 are recognizably closer to Shakespeare's in form, style, and even theme, than those of most other Elizabethans, with the exception of Drayton (who in his most 'Shakespearean' pieces may have been imitating Shakespeare). It has been argued that Daniel too was imitating Shakespeare, but the more traditional view has been that Shakespeare was indebted to Daniel.

We must also note the general affinity in verse and language between the Sonnets and *Venus and Adonis* (1593) and *Lucrece* (1594), as well as the parallel between the arguments of the first seventeen sonnets and Venus' attempt to persuade Adonis to 'use' his beauty. The ravages of Time is a topic shared by *Lucrece* with many of the Sonnets; but the sense of transience is strong also in many plays which are certainly later. Statistical methods have been applied to detailed resemblances between the Sonnets and the plays; such attempts at scientific measurement are of limited value in the study of human creations, but the cumulative evidence of various surveys puts the Sonnets with the plays of earlier composition. Statistics tend to confirm 'impressions', that is, our readiness to associate the poetry of the Sonnets with *Romeo and Juliet* and *Love's Labour's Lost* rather than *Measure for Measure*, with *King John* and *Richard II* rather than *Macbeth*.

Commentators like Samuel Butler and Leslie Hotson, who have sought to place the Sonnets chiefly in the late

1580s, have to explain away, not only the above considerations, but also the repeated statements that the poet is no longer young—whether they are joking (138) or earnest (73). Moreover, the easy mastery of rhetoric and verbal music in the great majority of the Sonnets would seem to relate them to the work of an artist who had already found himself, in his success as a dramatist in the early 1590s, rather than to the beginnings of a very youthful poet.

Attempts to date the Sonnets by means of real or supposed references to contemporary events have been unsuccessful, though 107 undoubtedly refers to the passing of what was felt to be a national crisis; those who have held the event to be the defeat of the Armada in 1588 have to disprove that it was the death of Queen Elizabeth, and the peaceful accession of King James, in 1603—or some other time of public anxiety and relief. In this connection it is a waste of time to consider the careers of Lord Southampton or Lord Pembroke, for there is no real evidence that either of them was in any way concerned in the composition or inspiration of the Sonnets.

The following dedication, signed with the initials of the publisher, was prefixed to the volume of 1609 (see frontispiece reproduction):

TO THE ONLIE BEGETTER OF
THESE INSUING SONNETS
MR. W. H. ALL HAPPINESSE
AND THAT ETERNITIE
PROMISED
BY
OUR EVER-LIVING POET
WISHETH
THE WELL-WISHING
ADVENTURER IN
SETTING
FORTH

T.T.

The natural interpretation of these words is that Mr W. H. had inspired the Sonnets, and was the young man whom, in so many of them, the poet says he hoped to immortalize.

As printed in 1609, the Sonnets fall into two sections, the first being much longer than the second. After a close inspection, we may well think that Shakespeare was responsible both for the broad division, and for the sequence of the poems within each series (though several of the poems in the second seem to be placed at random). The first series consists of one hundred and twenty-five sonnets, and ends with a piece of twelve lines in rhymed couplets, which is therefore not a sonnet, though numbered 126: it seems designed as an epilogue or *envoi* to a manuscript of the first series. Many of the preceding poems are plainly addressed to a young man; all of them would seem to express Shakespeare's thoughts and feelings for or about him. The twenty-eight sonnets of the second series are either addressed to, or can be associated with, a woman, a dark beauty whom Shakespeare speaks of as his mistress (and in terms which leave no doubt of the sense in which he uses the word). Among them even those which seem to stand apart from the others are nevertheless more appropriately placed here than in the first series. Thus the two 'moral' or 'penitential' sonnets, 129 and 146, in which Shakespeare parallels Sidney's two recantations in *Certain Sonnets*[1], occur in the context of poems that deal bitterly with physical desire (137, 147, and others); while the two trifling epigrams thrown in at the end are both compliments to 'my Mistress', and may perhaps have been written on a visit to Bath, in her company.

The two series can be linked by those sonnets in the first which present Shakespeare's friend as betraying him with his mistress (40, 41, 42, if not others), and by those in the second which appear to refer to the same situation (133-6 and 143, 144, 152).

Some editors have changed the order of 1609, either to substantiate their own views of the relationships between the

1 Printed in 1598.

poet, the friend and the mistress, or because they could not see any final significance in the existing order. Thus Samuel Butler transferred to the first series the sonnets in which Shakespeare writes of love as madness or disease, because he sought to degrade and darken the relationship with Mr W. H. Others have thought they could improve the effect by bringing together all the poems in which Shakespeare writes of absence or a journey, or debates his friend's integrity, or asserts his own faith and constancy. Yet such themes and occasions might be expected to recur at intervals, in a friendship of some duration. And if the poems are grouped together on such a principle, do we not rather assume, or gain the impression, that Shakespeare is writing a series of exercises on set themes, instead of taking his inspiration from a living friendship and changing circumstances? Still other editors and critics have rearranged the Sonnets to suit their own ideas of how love or friendship should evolve, or have found some verbal or technical principle, to produce a new pattern. No re-arrangement has proved to be generally acceptable.

In 1944, the editor of the Variorum Edition completed his survey of the comments of about a hundred and fifty years, and was led to conclude that the Sonnets had 'encouraged and fostered world-wide folly'; much of what has been written since confirms his judgement.[1] What passes for evidence and rational argument in criticism of the Sonnets would hardly pass for either in any other department of life. The absurdities are nearly always found in association with one, or both, of two ideas: the first, that most of the Sonnets are written to a 'patron', who is almost inevitably thought of as a great nobleman; the second, that some or all of them are purely 'literary', having no reference to real persons or events. Singly or together, these two notions can have only one effect: to remove the Sonnets from the

[1] See Rollins, Vol II, p. 399; and *The Riddle of Shakespeare's Sonnets*, ed. E. Hubler, 1962, *passim*.

realities of Shakespeare's private life. There can be little doubt that they were invented for that reason, and that they continue to appeal because they can still serve that purpose.

'Human kind cannot bear very much reality', says T. S. Eliot. Most scholars are afraid of the contents of the Sonnets because, if we take them at their face value, they tell us of Shakespeare's passionate devotion to a younger man— which must be suspect; and of his unwilling subjection to a woman whom he recognized to be worthless.

The method I have used in reading the Sonnets is to take them at their face value: to assume that they mean what they say, that Shakespeare is writing of his own emotions and experiences. I am quite aware that the truth of this assumption is not measurable, verifiable by experiment, or demonstrable by abstract reasoning; but I do not propose to repeat that point at every juncture, because it seems to me quite unimportant. The interpretation of works of art can never be a matter of rational or scientific demonstration, however much knowledge or method we may need on our way; to arrive at some understanding we need rather to draw upon the whole of our being, and have a feeling for reality which cannot be taken for granted.

The 'literary' hypothesis has never been supported by any effective external evidence; it is a mere evasion, and need not concern us further. The 'patron' theory will seem to many both more plausible and less controversial, since it may not seem necessarily to affect the reality of the emotions expressed. Yet in effect it always gives those emotions some unreality, as if 'love' must be understood to mean 'high esteem' or 'admiration' or 'grateful attachment', and should certainly not be thought of as a genuine passion, which might carry the suspicion of homosexual feeling. Now in this connection it is unnecessary, if we mean by homosexuality a physical relationship or desire: the Sonnets themselves are the best evidence that Shakespeare's love sought no physical consummation. On the other hand if the term is held to apply to an overwhelming attraction towards a person of the same sex as oneself, which aims at what used to be called an 'ideal' or 'passionate' friendship, we must nonetheless acknowledge that such emotions, and such an ideal, are what we find in the Sonnets. To this extent and in this way the experience they record is abnormal, for such emotions are common only in adolescence, and rare in later life.

On such an interpretation it may seem irrelevant whether the object of the poet's devotion is an unidentified Mr W. H. or an Elizabethan peer. But the social conditions of the time render most improbable a true intimacy between a man in Shakespeare's position, and such princelings as the Earls of Southampton and Pembroke. 'A plague on both your noble houses', one is tempted to exclaim. Their introduction into the question carries with it numberless possibilities of confusion and misunderstanding, born of our vain imaginations, snobbery, and tendency to glamourize history.

It will be said that Shakespeare speaks of the young man as his social superior. But any youth who was 'a gentleman born' would have had unquestionably a higher standing than Shakespeare, who spent his life in a despised profession, hoping only to make enough money and to acquire enough property to substantiate in the end his claim to gentility. The status of a gentleman was then clearly defined; what was required was 'good' birth, with or without inherited wealth.

Theory is perhaps like mud; throw enough of it, and some will stick. How else can one explain why many scholars continue to believe that Shakespeare's friend must have been his patron, and that patron either Southampton or Pembroke, when there is no convincing evidence for either? And how else can one understand their reluctance to accept Mr W. H. as one William Hughes, on the evidence of the poems themselves (20, 134, 135, 136)? Is it because they feel that, if they do, they must then choose between the William Hughes of Oscar Wilde and that of Samuel Butler? But both are creatures of the imagination, evolved by witty eccentrics, each with his axe to grind. Why should there not have been an unrecorded William Hughes, who would bear no resemblance to either?

Perhaps we can find a view of Shakespeare's relationship with both the young man and the dark beauty which will persuade people that we do not have to call in the English nobility in order to protext Shakespeare from 'an odious imputation'.[1]

Shakespeare's only reference to the dangerous subject is in Sonnet 20, and it is quite explicit. The poem has no other purpose than to declare that his love has no use for the young man's body; to say so jestingly, gracefully, with the licentious touches that Shakespeare always applies to sexual topics when he is in this mood; but to say it as plainly as possible. Yet this Sonnet only states openly what is implied both in Sonnet 144 later, and earlier in the first seventeen Sonnets, those on marriage and procreation.

Sonnets 1 to 17, with their persuasions to marriage, have been thought bizarre, or unintelligible: what man ever cared whether another man married or not, asks Mr C. S. Lewis?[2] But it is surely no accident, and far from irrelevant, that these love-poems should begin with a substantial group which establishes the masculinity of both the young man and the poet. Clearly Shakespeare was not unaware of how the friendship he desired might appear in the eyes of others, or of its object. These poems are the threshold to a special relationship.

Mr Leishman has remarked that the Sonnets are wholly free from the 'wooing' which is dominant in Renaissance and Petrarchan sonneteering; and this is true, if 'wooing' is defined as overt persuasion to the beloved to love the lover, and to demonstrate it in the most straight-forward manner. But compliments are themselves a form of wooing: extreme admiration and devotion, expressed with such power as Shakespeare expresses them, are certainly a bid for some

---

[1] Butler, *Shakespeare's Sonnets*, p. 77.
[2] *The Sixteenth Century (excluding Drama)*, Oxford (1954), p. 503.

corresponding attention or recognition. Even the eventual sublimity of Shakespeare's love, the generosity of the devotion he comes to feel and express, can be seen as an attempt (perhaps unconscious) to outbid all more ordinary, selfish, claims and devotions. The note of fervour is perhaps even heightened by a certain desperation: this is the poet's only claim, the only lever he has, with which to move his friend to return his love.

The presence of this indirect kind of wooing, as well as the reassurance they implicitly offer, is the best explanation of why the first seventeen sonnets should have been written at all, and especially of why they should have been written first. In urging the young man to perpetuate a unique beauty, Shakespeare has found a way in which his poetry can serve his passion: he demonstrates at once the degree of his admiration, his power to celebrate its object, and the purity of his motives. He offers adulation and devotion, but to one of whom he asks no more than to be allowed to offer them. If we are to believe him, he is not only willing, but anxious, that the youth should seek normal love and its fulfilment.

This is not to say that there was not, on the one hand, some immediate reality in the question of whether the young man would go in search of a wife: this would naturally be the wish of the family and friends of a youth who is setting out on life with great personal beauty, and exposed to obvious temptations. Nor would one deny, on the other hand, that Shakespeare's first and most urgent impulse is to express his delight in the young man's beauty:

> Who will believe my verse in time to come,
> If it were fill'd with your most high deserts?
> Though yet, Heaven knows, it is but as a tomb
> Which hides your life, and shows not half your parts.
> If I could write the beauty of your eyes,
> And in fresh numbers number all your graces,
> The age to come would say 'This Poet lies,
> Such heavenly touches ne'er touch'd earthly faces.'
> So should my papers (yellowed with their age)

> Be scorn'd, like old men of less truth than tongue,
> And your true rights be term'd a Poet's rage,
> Aud stretchèd metre of an antique song.
>   But were some child of yours alive that time,
>   You should live twice—in it, and in my rhyme.   (17)

The length at which the 'procreation' theme is treated, and its subsequent complete disappearance, tend to confirm that we have here a well-defined early phase in the friendship, after which there is a leap forward into greater intimacy: this may be measured in the next poems, 18 and 19, in which the poet's verse replaces procreation as a means of immortalization; and above all in 20, in which the youth has become 'the Master Mistress of my passion'.

It could be argued that even within these first twenty sonnets, we can see *in potentia* all the factors which are to determine the course of the emotions which follow. In Sonnet 20 the whole question of marriage has vanished, in the implied recognition that the youth is in fact more interested in amorous adventure. That perception, obvious in the change of tone, might be realistic enough; but what of the place Shakespeare forsees for himself, in the young man's exploration of love? 'Mine be thy love and thy love's use their [i.e. women's] treasure.' The Sonnet could not have been written except by a man who had accepted a dichotomy between the love of women, as he knew it, and his craving for complete emotional fulfilment. The attempt to find the latter in friendship, while the body and its demands are assumed to lead elsewhere, and do in fact lead to moral servitude, disgust and bitterness, is what we find recorded in the poet's dealings with his friend and his mistress respectively.

Consequently the last twenty-eight sonnets, though they have been called 'a disordered appendix', and reveal much that may offend and repel us, are no less important to our understanding of Shakespeare than the first series. Among them, 144 offers the most direct and concise statement of that opposition between physical and non-physical love, which is the key to the Sonnets:

Two loves I have, of comfort and despair,
Which like two spirits do suggest me still.
The better angel is a man right fair,
The worser spirit a woman colour'd ill.
To win me soon to hell, my female evil
Tempteth my better angel from my side,
And would corrupt my saint to be a devil,
Wooing his purity with her foul pride.
And whether that my angel be turn'd fiend,
Suspect I may, yet not directly tell;
But being both from me, both to each friend,
I guess one angel in another's hell.
Yet this shall I ne'er know, but live in doubt,
Till my bad angel fire my good one out.   (144)

The betrayal of the poet by his 'two loves' might be seen
by modern psychology as a confirmation of the dichotomy
in Shakespeare's emotional life; the young man would be as
it were impelled to his intrigue with the woman, by the
peculiar intensity of his bond with her lover. If we accept
the order of the first series, the episode comes fairly early
(34, 35 and 40, 42). Shakespeare condoned the fault in both
offenders (134-136, 143); but he makes no secret of what
brought him most pain, in the double betrayal:

That thou hast her, it is not all my grief,
And yet it may be said I lov'd her dearly;
That she hath thee is of my wailing chief,
A loss in love that touches me more nearly.   (42)

'Suns of the world may stain' (33): but the youth must and
will remain the focus of all Shakespeare's best hopes, the
longed-for possession that will compensate for all the stains
that have tarnished his life; while the mistress, however
powerful her present hold may be, is essentially but one of
those blots (142, 152). The theme of compensation is everywhere, in the sonnets of friendship:

> When, in disgrace with Fortune and men's eyes,
> I all alone beweep my outcast state,
> And trouble deaf heaven with my bootless cries,
> And look upon myself and curse my fate;
> Wishing me like to one more rich in hope,
> Featur'd like him, like him with friends possess'd,
> Desiring this man's art, and that man's scope,
> With what I most enjoy contented least:
> Yet in these thoughts myself almost despising,
> Haply I think on thee, and then my state,
> Like to the lark at break of day arising
> From sullen earth, sings hymns at Heaven's gate;
>    For thy sweet love remember'd such wealth brings,
>    That then I scorn to change my state with kings.  (29)

What we see is the further course, over a period of three years or more (104), of a relationship on which Shakespeare's romantic idealism had placed such a tremendous burden of significance.

The existing order of the first series at least gives a convincing impression of the ebb and flow of emotions involved in real life, and of new problems and meanings emerging from a relationship that, after all, cannot stand still. There are at least three absences, two clearly associated with journeys (27, 28, perhaps as far as 32; 43-45, perhaps including all as far as 52, or even 55; 97-99). There are well-defined groups springing out of incidents or new perceptions (33-36, perhaps as far as 39; 67-70; 71-74; 78-86; 91-96; 108-12 and 117-19). There are lapses of time, pauses and renewals: 26 reads like an *envoi* to a copy of the preceding poems; 55 is perhaps such another climax, followed by a pause indicated in the opening of 56. A similar pause is indicated by 100 and 101; and from that point of renewal, throughout several poems, Shakespeare is concerned, first, to assert that his love is unchanged, and next, to excuse a time in which he has appeared to neglect his friend for newer acquaintances. (By the way, can we imagine these poems as addressed to a patron?) Periodically Shakespeare

renews his vows—if indeed every sonnet is not to be
regarded as a re-enactment of his devotion. Sometimes (and
for the first time more than half way through the series) he
remarks on the inevitable monotony of his verses (76, 105,
108), and turns the observation to yet another tribute: it
must be realized that every sonnet in the sequence is ex-
plicitly a love-poem, and a compliment (with the possible
exception of 121).

The group of sonnets occasioned by the appearance of a
rival poet (78-86) is a clear instance of how Shakespeare
builds poems on changing circumstances, yet always directs
the poetry towards a re-assertion of love, and also to some
vision of love and poetry transcending time (in this group,
81). Soon after this, 91-96 seem to show particularly well
the way in which the poems grow organically out of one
another. We might almost imagine that the poet had before
him a manuscript of the series, and glanced at the last poem
in it as he prepared to write the next. Thus 91 is a natural
successor to 90, in so far as it expounds, with a renewal of
conviction, what the friend's love means to the poet: how
aware he is that at one stroke he may lose it, and all his
happiness. 92 is in the main a reply to the fear at the end of
91, yet ends with a new fear: 'Thou mayst be false, and yet I
know it not'. 93 develops this directly, in close argument
from 92. 94-96, though not so closely linked, flow out of the
final image of 93:

> How like Eve's apple doth thy beauty grow,
> If thy sweet virtue answer not thy show!

These last three poems are a mixture of tributes and warn-
ings, in which the youth's possible sensuality and levity (not
his chastity, as some modern critics absurdly assume) are seen
as a blot on his beauty: 'Lilies that fester smell far worse than
weeds' (94). Whether this tone was unwelcome does not
appear; but we may note that there is a break in the series
after 96, and that the young man's 'truth' or purity is never
again questioned.

Sonnet 121 closes a sequence (beginning with 107), in which Shakespeare is concerned to excuse his recent apparent neglect (109, 110), explaining that it was meant to test his true love by means of inferior friendships (110, 117, 118); these would reveal its full glory by contrast (119). 121 seems an overflow from this self-defence, with its feelings of revulsion and self-criticism—an overflow which takes a different, and possibly unintended, direction. Does Shakespeare stumble into a perception that his friend's reproaches (implied in preceding sonnets) are not far removed from the imputations of vulgar minds which do not know him so well? Is he discouraged to realize that even now his friend understands him so little? Is there also a sudden suspicion that all these outsiders (including the friend) may perhaps be right, that there may be a taint in all his friendships, perhaps of original sin, perhaps of something more sinister? If such a suspicion intrudes, as it seems to do in the couplet, it may be the reason why the sonnet fails to become a compliment, where others have succeeded; why the sequence lapses here for a while; and why it comes to an end shortly afterwards.

The last poems are a final illustration of how the Sonnets grow out of sometimes trivial, even uncomfortable, situations, into exalted affirmation. 122 excuses Shakespeare for having given away a gift from his friend, one of those notebooks or 'tablets' referred to also in 77. Its admirable rhetoric and tone cannot wholly disguise the somewhat sad fact that sets them off. As a result Shakespeare continues with the theme he has devised, of love transcending time; and produces three poems of metaphysical force and complex metaphor, in which constant love defies change and outward show. (The 'suborned Informer' of the last couplet would, on this view, be the 'Time' of 123.)

Such a summary or description as I have attempted—indeed any summary, however full or careful—cannot but seem to reduce the Sonnets to something less than themselves. Shakespeare's poetry transforms whatever he has to say: what he says in fact seems to take in all life and experience, and to go beyond life, to point beyond it to what cannot be known, but only believed or prophesied. Here is indeed one of the most potent recurrent themes of the Sonnets:

> Let me not to the marriage of true minds
> Admit impediments. Love is not love
> Which alters when it alteration finds,
> Or bends with the remover to remove.
> O no, it is an ever-fixèd mark
> That looks on tempests and is never shaken;
> It is the star to every wand'ring bark,
> Whose worth's unknown, although his height be taken.
> Love's not Time's fool, though rosy lips and cheeks
> Within his bending sickle's compass come.
> Love alters not with his brief hours and weeks,
> But bears it out even to the edge of doom:
>    If this be error, and upon me proved,
>    I never writ, nor no man ever loved. (116)

But can we respond fully to this passionate eloquence, unless we are ready to believe that it sprang out of day-to-day experience?

## SONNETS (ii)

In the Sonnets Shakespeare applied the kind of poetry he had displayed in *Venus and Adonis* and *Lucrece* to the demands of his own experience. The exigencies of life gave him a motive and an urgency which are only too obviously missing in the two longer poems; and as a result, the appreciation of the Sonnets as only exquisitely wrought language —though this they certainly are—must leave us unsatisfied.

I have so far been concerned chiefly with the historical facts about the Sonnets, and with a context of personal relationships which I feel to be essential to our apprehension of them. In turning now to look at them rather as poems, I do not see how it is possible to exclude such ideas as I have outlined already. For Shakespeare's poetic genius—his whole sensibility and imagination and marvellous range of utterance—not only transforms the meaning of the personal history: it may be said truly, at least of his relationship with the young man, that the personal history could never have come into being except through his own imagination.

> What is your substance, whereof are you made,
> That millions of strange shadows on you tend?

asks the poet (53), who himself brings to the living human creature those endless vibrations, and the aching sense of its beauty and mystery. Despite all the painful questionings and explorings that underlie so many of the first series, the Sonnets, even more than most love-poems, are poems of enjoyment; of what Keats called 'luxury', the absorbed contemplation of beauty:

> When in the chronicle of wasted time,
> I see descriptions of the fairest wights,
> And beauty making beautiful old rhyme,
> In praise of ladies dead, and lovely knights:
> Then in the blazon of sweet beauty's best,
> Of hand, of foot, of lip, of eye, of brow,
> I see their antique pen would have express'd
> Even such a beauty as you master now.
> So all their praises are but prophecies
> Of this our time, all you prefiguring,
> And for they look'd but with divining eyes,
> They had not skill enough your worth to sing;
> For we which now behold these present days,
> Have eyes to wonder, but lack tongues to praise.   (106)

In two sonnets (113, 114), Shakespeare transcribes his experience of obsession, asking himself whether it is not a form of intoxication, actual poisoning. The poetry is here decidedly less powerful than in many other pieces; but when Shakespeare speaks of 'my mind being crown'd with you' and says of his sense of enjoyment, 'And my great mind most kingly drinks it up' (114), we have the plainest statement of this aspect of his love.

The enjoyment of beauty is fused with Shakespeare's delight in creating beauty as he writes. Shakespeare must have lived through his art, and probably never felt more himself than in its exercise. It is no derogation from his 'sincerity' to say that he constantly endeavours, and delights, to say the perfect thing: perfect both in its form and in its appropriateness. His delight in his own power is most obvious when he treats the theme of immortalization, traced so perceptively by Mr J. B. Leishman:

> Not marble, nor the gilded monuments
> Of princes, shall outlive this powerful rhyme;
> But you shall shine more bright in these contents
> Than unswept stone, besmear'd with sluttish time.
> When wasteful wars shall statues overturn,
> And broils root out the work of masonry,
> Nor Mars his sword, nor war's quick fire shall burn
> The living record of your memory.
> 'Gainst death, and all oblivious enmity
> Shall you pace forth; your praise shall still find room,
> Even in the eyes of all posterity
> That wear this world out to the ending doom.
>   So till the judgement, that yourself arise,
>     You live in this, and dwell in lovers' eyes.  (55)

> Since brass, nor stone, nor earth, nor boundless sea,
> But sad mortality o'ersways their power,
> How with this rage shall beauty hold a plea,
> Whose action is no stronger than a flower?
> O how shall summer's honey breath hold out,
> Against the wrackful siege of batt'ring days,
> When rocks impregnable are not so stout,
> Nor gates of steel so strong, but Time decays?
> O fearful meditation, where alack,
> Shall Time's best jewel from Time's chest lie hid?
> Or what strong hand can hold his swift foot back,
> Or who his spoil of beauty can forbid?
>   O none, unless this miracle have might,
>     That in black ink my love may still shine bright.  (65)

But this consciousness of golden utterance, and worthy celebration of beauty, shows only half of his delight in saying the right thing. The right, the perfect thing, turns out more and more to be the handsome thing: the generosity with which he forgives a fault, the self-effacement with which he will love, the gratitude with which he will accept what is granted, the humility with which he will exculpate himself. Thus, in the episode of the rival poet (78-86), Shakespeare may have felt some jealousy; but surely he enjoys the situation, and the opportunities it offers him of showing his courtesy, modesty, generous love and constancy? It seems impossible that, after writing as he often had of his own verse, he should have been wholly sincere in praise of his rival's (80, 85, 86); but this was the only handsome line to take. While he acknowledges defeat in the poetic contest, Shakespeare in every piece turns his argument to a compliment to his friend; and this exercise in generosity leads up to one of the greatest outbursts of renunciation, a surrender so passionate that it must surely be a moral victory:

> Farewell, thou art too dear for my possessing,
> And like enough thou knowst thy estimate.
> The charter of thy worth gives thee releasing;
> My bonds in thee are all determinate.
> For how do I hold thee but by thy granting,
> And for that riches where is my deserving?
> The cause of this fair gift in me is wanting,
> And so my patent back again is swerving.
> Thyself thou gav'st, thy own worth then not knowing,
> Or me to whom thou gav'st it, else mistaking;
> So thy great gift upon misprision growing,
> Comes home again, on better judgement making.
>   Thus have I had thee as a dream doth flatter:
>   In sleep a king, but waking, no such matter.   (87)

Whether or not Shakespeare felt he had been outbidden in praise, the mere fact that another poet's rivalry could assume such importance, precipitate such a throng of feelings, and occasion so many poems, points to another way in which we may observe the relation between Shakespeare's poetry and his passion.

⸎ More than most love-poets, at least in the sonnet tradition, Shakespeare writes directly *to* or *for* the object of his love: if he also writes of what his love 'means' to him (the staple of so much Petrarchan verse), still he writes it for his friend's perusal, not solely as a discipline or discharge of his own emotions, or a meditation *sub specie aeternitatis*. One sign of this is that there are in the first series no sonnets to third persons, such as those written by Petrarch and his followers, referring to their love. Another appears in a comparison of the first with the second series, where several sonnets speak *of* the mistress (130, 138, 144): in two of the most powerful she has disappeared (129, 146); and in most of those nominally addressed to her, the function of the poetry is clearly to relieve Shakespeare's feelings rather than to assure her of his love: it is hard to believe that some were intended for her eyes (e.g. 131, 137, 147, 148).

But throughout the first series the poetry itself was, and had to be, a function of the friendship, its chief instrument, the very proof of its existence. Without it the bond perhaps had never existed; and it becomes the currency of a love that can make no demands, and find hardly any other means of expression: 'Since why to love, I can allege no cause' (49). Hence so many intensely poetic declarations of selfless devotion, in which the *statement* of devotion, like the devotion itself, becomes the source of satisfaction:

> Being your slave, what should I do but tend
> Upon the hours and times of your desire?
> I have no precious time at all to spend,
> Nor services to do, till you require.
> Nor dare I chide the world-without-end hour,
> Whilst I (my sovereign) watch the clock for you,
> Nor think the bitterness of absence sour,
> When you have bid your servant once adieu.
> Nor dare I question with my jealous thought,

> Where you may be, or your affairs suppose,
> But like a sad slave stay and think of nought
> Save where you are, how happy you make those.
>    So true a fool is love, that in your Will,
>    Though you do anything, he thinks no ill.  (57)

Some of the formal qualities of the Sonnets can be related closely to this one of their functions. Since they are written *to* or *for* one person, they have in an unusual degree the tones of the speaking voice:

> No longer mourn for me when I am dead,
> Than you shall hear the surly sullen bell
> Give warning to the world that I am fled
> From this vile world, with vilest worms to dwell.
> Nay, if you read this line, remember not
> The hand that writ it, for I love you so,
> That I in your sweet thoughts would be forgot,
> If thinking on me then should make you woe.
> O if, I say, you look upon this verse,
> When I (perhaps) compounded am with clay,
> Do not so much as my poor name rehearse,
> But let your love even with my life decay;
>    Lest the wise world should look into your moan,
>    And mock you with me after I am gone.  (71)

Here, however intimate the tone, we hear the deliberate inflections of the voice rising and falling, the throb of emotion springing up in a man's voice as he speaks.

Such inflections and intonations become an obvious, regular part of the total pattern. The rhyme-scheme of the Shakespearean sonnet lends itself directly to this kind of vocal writing. The speaker can set out with a theme proclaimed in the first quatrain, elaborate it in the next two, and clinch the whole with the couplet:

> That time of year thou mayst in me behold,
> When yellow leaves, or none, or few, do hang
> Upon those boughs which shake against the cold,

Bare ruin'd choirs where late the sweet birds sang.
In me thou seest the twilight of such day,
As after sunset fadeth in the west,
Which by and by black night doth take away,
Death's second self, that seals up all in rest.
In me thou seest the glowing of such fire,
That on the ashes of his youth doth lie,
As the death-bed whereon it must expire,
Consum'd with that which it was nourish'd by.
   This thou perceiv'st, which makes thy love more strong,
   To love that well, which thou must leave ere long.  (73)

Finally in this connection, we see that the Sonnets are essentially the poems of a dramatist. Their function as repeated declarations, protestations of love, varied and adjusted to changing circumstances, enables Shakespeare to write each of them as he would write a speech in a play. He hears the poem spoken as he writes, and it is conceived as a statement of a fancy or impulse in a given situation, a unit opening with some reference to what has just happened, or been said, then unfolding to a full response—whether it is to end with the point of greatest emphasis, or be rounded off with some phrases of dismissal:

O never say that I was false of heart,
Though absence seem'd my flame to qualify!
As easy might I from myself depart,
As from my soul, which in thy breast doth lie.
That is my home of love; if I have rang'd,
Like him that travels I return again,
Just to the time, not with the time exchang'd;
So that myself bring water for my stain.
Never believe, though in my nature reign'd
All frailties that besiege all kinds of blood,
That it could so preposterously be stain'd,
To leave for nothing all thy sum of good;
   For nothing this wide universe I call,
   Save thou, my Rose; in it thou art my all.  (109)

How like a winter hath my absence been
From thee, the pleasure of the fleeting year!
What freezings have I felt, what dark days seen!
What old December's bareness everywhere!
And yet this time remov'd was summer's time,
The teeming autumn big with rich increase,
Bearing the wanton burthen of the prime,
Like widow'd wombs after their lord's decease.
Yet this abundant issue seem'd to me
But hope of orphans, and unfather'd fruit;
For summer and his pleasures wait on thee,
And thou away, the very birds are mute;
   Or if they sing, 'tis with so dull a cheer,
   That leaves look pale, dreading the winter's near.   (97)

It may be also the dramatist's gift and practice that give Shakespeare's style its immense *authority*: that resounding force of expression which not only strengthens the straight-forward, but gives persuasiveness to poems which one may judge to be less assured, or even confused. Even in such cases (e.g. in 69, 70, 94 or 121) the final impression becomes one of what we may call *authentic* confusion, the confusion of strong emotions and conceptions which have not yet clarified themselves, not of obscure or feeble artifice.

Shakespeare's use of the sonnet is directed mostly towards the imaginative enjoyment of love and life; the more complex and less successful sonnets are on the whole those into which some intractably painful element has entered. Hence the proportion of jarring pieces is large only in the second series, which is the *enfer* of the book. Undertones of suffering and discord are certainly to be found in the first hundred and twenty-six sonnets. But here Shakespeare was putting together 'friendship's garland'; and despite his questionings of the young man's true nature, and his pushing to the limit the scope of self-sacrifice, there is scarcely a poem which is not meant to please. Even 94 is intended as yet another celebration of beauty, while 95 and 96 show the gentleness with which Shakespeare could warn, or reprove.

The last half-dozen pieces, and particularly the *envoi*, may seem a disappointing conclusion, despite the re-asserted challenge to change, and vow of devotion. But after some of the earlier triumphs of these themes (104, 107 or 116), it was hardly possible to avoid a falling-off. The comparatively lower level of the last pieces seems another confirmation the the order of the Sonnets is chronological: if Shakespeare had been placing them arbitrarily, he could easily have ended on a higher note.

The order of the second series carries less conviction, but the nature of the relationships is plainer, the range of emotions is narrower, and there is no ambiguity about the final impression. The element of pain which was an undercurrent in the preceding poems, consistently channelled into a willing or exultant tribute, is here the dominating force; the lover chafes in shame or unwilling servitude:

> My love is as a fever longing still,
> For that which longer nurseth the disease,
> Feeding on that which doth preserve the ill,
> Th'uncertain sickly appetite to please:
> My reason, the physician to my love,
> Angry that his prescriptions are not kept,
> Hath left me, and I desperate now approve
> Desire is death, which physic did except.
> Past cure I am, now reason is past care,
> And frantic-mad with evermore unrest;
> My thoughts and my discourse as madmen's are,
> At random from the truth vainly express'd;
>   For I have sworn thee fair, and thought thee bright,
>   Who art as black as hell, as dark as night. (147)

The willingness Shakespeare has already shown to acquiesce in the sufferings others can bring him, is apparent again, but in a more startling form: more tormented, more aware of self-abasement (135, 136, 141, 143 and others). Apart from the trivialities of 145, 153, and 154, a few poems are charming compliments, fanciful in the manner of *Love's Labour's Lost* or *A Midsummer Night's Dream* (127, 128, 132). Yet the praises of 'black beauty' are neighbours to some in which the woman's dark complexion takes on a more sinister meaning (131). Like Sidney, Shakespeare rejects poetic artifice in compliment: 130 is a companion and contrast to 21. Yet the first poem has no such hints of the physical 'facts of life' and even less the tone of sustained, rather brutal, jesting.

Evidently the love of woman, for Shakespeare, is predominantly physical, and unrewarding at that; and it is in these poems that love in the form of physical desire is dismissed (129), and the soul urged to turn to spiritual realities (146). There are no such recantations in the poems of friendship. Shakespeare's love for his friend has the aspiration, the thirst for perfection, the worship of truth and beauty, of the Platonic tradition. But it is oddly lacking in the sense of the supernatural, the Christian hope, which was fundamental in Renaissance Platonism. Mr Leishman has brought out the absence of any sense of the after-life, of personal immortality, which so intense a devotion might have seemed likely to awaken. The sonnets of friendship will 'bear it out even to the edge of doom' (119). Beyond this indeed comes the resurrection of the body, in a sonnet which may have been intended as a provisional close or climax:

> So till the judgement, that yourself arise,
> You live in this, and dwell in lovers' eyes.  (55)

But even when the poet sees the world most plainly in the scale of eternal values, he is reluctant to accept death as a release, because it parts him from his love:

> Tired with all these, for restful death I cry:
> As to behold desert a beggar born,
> And needy nothing trimm'd in jollity,
> And purest faith unhappily forsworn,
> And gilded honour shamefully misplac'd,
> And maiden virtue rudely strumpeted,
> And right perfection wrongfully disgrac'd,

And strength by limping sway disabled,
And art made tongue-tied by authority,
And folly, doctor-like, controlling skill,
And simple truth miscall'd simplicity,
And captive good attending captain ill.
   Tired with all these, from these I would be gone,
   Save that to die, I leave my love alone. (66)

If we accept the Sonnets as a record of certain phases of Shakespeare's experience, there is much that will be a stumbling block to modern readers (though one may wonder whether there is anything here very different from, or more disturbing than, the love-poems of Catullus). In so unusual a relationship as that recorded in the first series, there is much that may give scandal or dismay: an apparent excess of emotion over what seem to be the facts; a tendency to self-abasement and self-depreciation, which seems unworthy in a man of Shakespeare's genius; a persistent attempt to wring satisfaction out of ingenious or wilful thinking, where a true emotional recompense was probably wanting. Throughout it may seem that the poet is trying to live in a fool's paradise, abusing his talent to create a dream-world which constantly crumbles, and has constantly to be repaired. In the second series there may seem to be a greater recognition of reality; but Shakespeare's relationship with his mistress in some ways parallels that with his friend. There is the same tendency to sophistry (135, 136), the same self-torment and self-abasement, with an even greater measure of emotional turmoil.

All these vivid realities testify to the psychological insecurity, an emotional 'immaturity'and 'unbalance', which is the very opposite of the norms and values held by many modern critics. Students may be swayed by an ideal of 'integration' or 'maturity' deriving from such writers as D. H. Lawrence and T. S. Eliot—who themselves were least provided with it, and whose genius depended on their not having it. The Sonnets only tell us that Shakespeare was of the same kidney. Like all great poetry, the Sonnets strive towards order and mastery of life; but the poet is impelled towards that reality and sanity by powerful forces of disorder within himself. Nowadays we take it for granted that in the plays Shakespeare stubbornly seeks some sovereign vision, or delicate point of balance. The Sonnets tell us more directly of the depths of violent emotion and conflict on which he drew for the shaping and reshaping of his dramas.

The fact that most of the Sonnets are inspired by masculine friendship, not by 'the love of women', gives them their special generosity and pathos—and even (as I have maintained) their eloquence. It may also explain why Shakespeare was able to raise the Renaissance form of sonnet to a new level of sublimity. Medieval faith and thought had given the Petrarchan sonnet its original moral beauty; the Renaissance had been unable to revive this, or carry it further; indeed the new emphasis on artistry and more worldly elements had seriously weakened it. But Shakespeare brings a new idealism —nothing abstract, but the beat and glow of intense emotion striving to grasp a new hope, a new discipline. His love-poetry is more liberated, yet more exacting—more spiritual, yet less secure: in a word, more *tragic*, than that of the long medieval and Renaissance tradition to which it belongs.

## IV.  *A LOVER'S COMPLAINT*

It is odd that *A Lover's Complaint*, which Malone called 'this beautiful poem, in every part of which the hand of Shakespeare is visible', should have been regarded by some recent writers as of doubtful authorship. The latest scholar to condemn it with a flourish was C. S. Lewis. Yet for many if not most critics, it carries its authorship on its face, being full of beauties of imagery, language and feeling that are, if not Shakespeare's, the work of an incredibly skilful plagiarist of his style. The language is more compressed and strained, the syntax more complex and obscure, than in *Venus* and *Lucrece;* but the poem was printed fifteen years after them, and can be presumed to have been written at least some years later. Shakespeare's style in his plays certainly moved in the direction of the greater idiosyncrasy and abruptness we find here. Surely all we need remark is that these stylistic developments are more successful in dramatic blank verse than in the rhymed stanzas of *A Lover's Complaint*, which no one will deny is on the whole unsatisfying, being perhaps a fragment.

If stylistic considerations are not, and cannot be, conclusive (as the debate seems to show), the content of the poem might persuade us that only Shakespeare could have written it. Here one may conjecture that its association with the Sonnets, and therefore with the wilderness of biographical theories about the Sonnets, has served to confuse the issue. Putting aside all misguided attempts to identify the forsaken maid and the fickle youth, one should be able to see in these persons and their story the true Shakespearean sensibility, and some of its preoccupations: youth, beauty and temptation; truth and deception in love; the hypnotic fascination of human personality. Above all it may be significant that the fascination of personality, of youth, beauty, and falsehood, is here all concentrated in the character of the young man, the faithless lover:

> Small show of man was yet upon his chin,
> His phoenix down began but to appear
> Like unshorn velvet, on that termless skin,
> Whose bare out-bragg'd the web it seem'd to wear . . .

> His qualities were beauteous as his form,
> For maiden-tongu'd he was and thereof free;
> Yet if men mov'd him, was he such a storm
> As oft 'twixt May and April is to see,
> When winds breathe sweet, unruly though they be.
>     His rudeness so with his authoriz'd youth
>     Did livery falseness in a pride of truth. (92-105)

In him a plenitude of subtle matter,
Applied to cautels, all strange forms receives,
Of burning blushes, or of weeping water,
Or swooning paleness; and he takes and leaves,
In either's aptness, as it best deceives:
    To blush at speeches rank, to weep at woes,
    Or to turn white and swoon at tragic shows.   (302-8)

If such a delight in the brilliance and mystery of human
character is compared with what we find in the plays, and
what is revealed in the Sonnets, one can hardly doubt the
attribution to Shakespeare. Add to this some other links with
the Sonnets, such as the youth's coldness, his indifference
towards his many loves (cf. Sonnet 94), and his offering their
gifts and tokens as a proof that they are all transcended by
his new love (Sonnets 31, 41); and one must conclude that
the general neglect of *A Lover's Complaint* is unjustified. For
all its charm of detail and its force of expression, it is indeed
in some way constricted, incomplete, and rather baffling:
we miss a clear motive, or focus of interest. But even its
incidental beauties are beyond the reach of most Elizabethan
poets; and its value as a document has been strangely
neglected.

## V.   *THE PHOENIX AND TURTLE*

Even in the nineteenth century, when the Sonnets began to
be taken seriously, *The Phoenix and Turtle* was neglected; but
in our time it has become one of the most admired of Shakespeare's poems, benefitting from the change of taste which
has brought Metaphysical poetry back into favour. It is
cryptic and oracular in tone: much of its power lies in its
mysteriousness, which is heightened by its appearance of
being an isolated, unexplained creation. Yet the circumstances
in which it was printed may help us to a glimpse of
Shakespeare's imagination at work, without diminishing
our wonder at the poem he achieved.

A miscellaneous volume called *Loves Martyr*, written by one Robert Chester, and printed in 1601, contains an appendix of poems, some signed, some unsigned: of these Shakespeare's is the fifth; it is signed, but bears no title. Other pieces are signed by Ben Jonson, Chapman, and Marston; all are based upon, or linked to, the love and death of the Phoenix and the Turtle, which is related in the body of the book. There it serves to frame or hold together a poetical farrago, including such elements as the story of King Arthur, some British and English history, a herbal, and a treatise on precious stones; yet in itself it is no less incoherent, indeed absurd. Nature brings together the Phoenix, which is female, and a Turtle dove, which is male, in order that they may die together, and another Phoenix rise from their ashes. Both birds are evidently allegories of human lovers, probably living persons.

Shakespeare has paid no great attention to the details of Chester's myth; for instance, he denies the two birds their promised offspring. He has taken them as an emblem of passion consummated in death, and concentrated on the beauty of their sublime and absolute union:

> So they lov'd, as love in twain
> Had the essence but in one:
> Two distincts, division none;
> Number there in love was slain. (25-28)

The Phoenix is the incarnation of Beauty, the Turtle of Truth; by their death, the world is bereft of both:

> Truth may seem, but cannot be;
> Beauty brag, but 'tis not she;
> Truth and beauty buried be. (62-64)

An intense delight in faithful love is combined with a sense of doom, and a longing for the peace of death:

> Death is now the Phoenix' nest,
> And the Turtle's loyal breast
> To eternity doth rest. (56-58)

Here are themes that are latent in the Sonnets, but which never found there the triumphant, exulting expression that they are given in this poem of fantasy. Can one see a parallel between the affirmations of *The Phoenix and Turtle* and Shakespeare's last plays, a few years later? Both here and there the dominant idea seems to be that of reconciliation, an achieved unity of spirit, a faith asserted after loss or sorrow; and in both the poem and the Romances the assertion seems to be made possible only by an element of fantasy. By some form of the supernatural, by magic or pagan religion, love is enabled to transcend nature and reason. C. S. Lewis has pointed out that the function of reason in *The Phoenix and Turtle* is to acknowledge what is beyond itself, to accept the paradox that 'Love hath reason, reason none' (47).

The organization of the poem is simple but powerful. It passes from the summoning of the birds to attend the funeral rites, to the singing of 'the anthem', which celebrates the mystery of two being fused into one; and then allots to Reason the final 'Threne'; for this the verse takes on a quicker beat, though it remains charged with solemn meanings. The poem comes to a close by rising, spreading its wings and taking flight.

Like some of the songs in the plays, *The Phoenix and Turtle* is an incantation, but longer, more sustained and intellectual. It creates a self-contained world, yet one with countless mysterious associations. The gathering of the birds brings overtones of folklore; the co-existence and identity of the lovers is expounded in terms which recall scholastic philosophy and medieval theology. There is an under-current of courtly Platonism. It is not surprising that some have thought that Shakespeare was here writing a poem deliberately in the Metaphysical manner, though his lyrical and rhapsodic use of the language of the schoolmen is very different from anything in Donne. The final impression is wholly Shakespearean: the freshness of language and imagery, the deep and overflowing human feeling.

The circumstances which gave rise to the poem will probably remain obscure: *Loves Martyr* and its appendix suggest that Chester's absurd but charming myth had tickled the fancy of Ben Jonson and his friends, who may have been approached to write commendatory verses, but ended by co-operating in an half-humorous, half-serious elaboration of the theme, or rather a comment on its quaintness. Shakespeare's is the only contribution which completely re-creates the central subject. To us his poem seems to have come out of the depths of his being; we can hardly mistake the life it draws from his feeling for pure, devoted love. He may have begun it as a freak of fancy; but if so, it took on a life of its own, and spoke with a new voice things which he found no means of saying in his other, direct and personal, love-poetry.

# SHAKESPEARE: THE POEMS

## A Select Bibliography

(Books published in London, unless stated otherwise)

### ABBREVIATIONS

| | |
|---|---|
| EC | *Essays in Criticism* |
| EETS | *Early English Text Society* |
| ELH | *English Literary History* |
| ES | *English Studies* |
| ESEA | *Essays and Studies by Members of the English Association* |
| JEGP | *Journal of English and Germanic Philology* |
| MLN | *Modern Language Notes* |
| MLR | *Modern Language Review* |
| MP | *Modern Philology* |
| PBSA | *Publications of the Bibliographical Society of America* |
| PMLA | *Publications of the Modern Language Association of America* |
| PQ | *Philological Quarterly* |
| RES | *Review of English Studies* |
| SAB | *Shakespeare Association Bulletin* |
| ScR | *Scrutiny* |
| SEL | *Studies in English Literature* (Rice University) |
| SeR | *Sewanee Review* |
| ShJ | *Shakespeare Jahrbuch* |
| ShQ | *Shakespeare Quarterly* |
| ShS | *Shakespeare Survey* |
| SP | *Studies in Philology* |
| TLS | *Times Literary Supplement* |
| UTSE | *University of Texas Studies in English* |

## GENERAL CRITICISM

DRAKE, N. *Shakespeare and his times*. 2 vols, 1817.

SAINTSBURY, G. 'Shakespeare: poems,' in *The Cambridge history of English literature*, V, 1910, pp. 223-35.

WYNDHAM, G. 'Poems of Shakespeare', in *Essays in Romantic literature*, 1919, pp. 237-88.

COURTHOPE, W. J. 'The lyrical element in Shakespeare's plays', in *A History of English poetry*, IV, 1922, pp. 19-53.

49

KELLETT, E. E. *Suggestions*, 1923.

CHAMBERS, E. K. *William Shakespeare: a study of facts and problems*, 1930, Vol. I, pp. 543-76.

RYLANDS, G. H. W. *Words and Poetry*, 1930.

RYLANDS, G. H. W. 'English Poetry and the Abstract Word', *ESEA*, XVI, 1930.

BALDWIN, T. W. *On the literary genetics of Shakespeare's poems and sonnets;* Urbana, 1950.

MURRY, J. Middleton. 'Shakespeare's dedication', in *John Clare and other studies*, 1950, pp. 45-57.

BRADBROOK, M. C. *Shakespeare and Elizabethan poetry*, 1951; reprinted 1964.

CRUTTWELL, P. *The Shakespearean moment and its place in the poetry of the seventeenth century*, 1954.

LEWIS, C. S. 'Verse in the "golden period"', in *The Sixteenth century (excluding drama)*, 1954, pp. 464-535.

KNIGHT, G. Wilson. *The mutual flame: on Shakespeare's Sonnets and 'The Phoenix and the Turtle'*, 1955.

SISSON, C. J. *New readings in Shakespeare*, 1956, Vol. I, pp. 207-8.

BULLOUGH, G. (ed.) *Narrative and dramatic sources of Shakespeare, Vol. I. Early comedies, poems, Romeo and Juliet*, 1957.

BROWN, J. R. and HARRIS, B. (eds.) *Stratford-upon-Avon studies, II: Elizabethan poetry*, 1960.

LEVER, J. W. 'The poems.' *ShS*, XV, 1962, 18-30.

MINCOFF, M. 'The chronology of Shakespeare's early work', *Zeitschrift fur Anglistik und Amerikanistik*, XI, 1963, 173-83.

## VENUS AND ADONIS

*First edition:* First printed 1593. Facsimiles ed. A. Symons (1886); ed. S. Lee (1905); Elizabethan Club (1964).

*Modern editions:* Ed. G. Wyndham (1898); Arden, ed. C. K. Pooler (1911. 2nd ed., 1928); Yale, ed. A. Feuillerat (1927); New Temple, ed, M. R. Ridley (1935); New Variorum, ed. E. H. Rollins (1938); New Arden, ed. F. T. Prince (1960); ed. O. S. Campbell (1964); ed. E. Hubler (1964); New Cambridge, ed. J. C. Maxwell (1966).

### CRITICAL STUDIES

BROWN, C. 'Shakespeare and the horse', *Library*, 3rd. Ser, III, 1912, 152-220.

SPENCER, H. 'Shakespeare's use of Golding in Venus and Adonis', *MLN*, XLIV, 1929, 435-7.

FORREST, H. T. S. *The original Venus and Adonis*, 1930.

PUTNEY, R. *'Venus and Adonis:* Amour with humor', *PQ*, XX, 1941, 533-48.

PRICE, H. T. 'The function of imagery in *Venus and Adonis*', *Papers of Michigan Academy of Science, Arts and Letters*, XXXI, 1945, 275-97.

HATTO, A. T. *'Venus and Adonis*—and the boar', *MLR*, XLI, 1946, 353-61.

MILLER, R. P. 'Venus, Adonis and the horses', *ELH*, XIX, 1952, 249-64.

PUTNEY, R. 'Venus Agonistes', *University of Colorado Studies in Language and Literature*, IV, 1953, 52-66.

PARTRIDGE, A. C. 'Shakespeare's orthography in *Venus and Adonis* and some early Quartos', *ShS*, VII, 1954, 35-47.

JACKSON, R. S. 'Narrative and imagery in Shakespeare's *Venus and Adonis*', *Papers of the Michigan Academy of Science, Arts and Letters*, XLIII, 1958, 315-20.

ALLEN, D. C. 'On *Venus and Adonis*', in DAVIS, H. & GARDNER, H. (eds.) *Elizabethan and Jacobean studies presented to F. P. Wilson*, 1959, pp. 100-11.

BONJOUR, A. 'From Shakespeare's Venus to Cleopatra's cupids', *ShS*, XV, 1962, 73-80.

BRADBROOK, M. 'Beasts and gods: Green's Groats-worth of Witte and the social purpose of *Venus and Adonis*', *ShS*, XV, 1962, 62-71.

LEVER, J. W. 'Venus and the second chance', *ShS*, XV, 1962, 81-88.

MILLER, R. P. 'The myth of Mars' hot minion in *Venus and Adonis' ELH*, XXVI, 1959, 470-81.

HAMILTON, A. C. *'Venus and Adonis'*, *SEL*, I, 1961, 1-15.

PALMATIER, M. A. 'A suggested new source in Ovid's *Metamorphoses* for Shakespeare's *Venus and Adonis*', *Huntington Library Quarterly*, XXIV, 1961, 163-9.

BUSH, D. 'Shakespeare: *Venus and Adonis* and *Lucrece*', in BUSH, D. *Mythology and the Renaissance tradition in English poetry;* rev. ed., New York, 1963, pp. 137-55.

CANTELUPE, E. B. 'An iconographical interpretation of *Venus and Adonis*, Shakespeare's Ovidian comedy', *ShQ*, XIV, 1963, 141-51.

BUTLER, C. and FOWLER, A. 'Time beguiling sport: number symbolism in Shakespeare's *Venus and Adonis*', in BLOOM, E. A. ed. *Shakespeare, 1564-1964;* Providence, 1964, pp. 124-33.

BOWERS, R. H. 'Anagnorisis or the shock of recognition in Shakespeare's *Venus and Adonis*', *Renaissance Papers*, 1962, 3-8.

BUXTON, J. 'Shakespeare: *Venus and Adonis*', in BUXTON, J. *Elizabethan taste*, 1964, pp. 295-306.

MUIR, K. '*Venus and Adonis*: comedy or tragedy', in THALER, A. and SANDERS, N. eds. *Shakespearean essays*'; Knoxville, 1964, pp. 1-14.

LEECH, C. 'Venus and her nun: portraits of women in love by Shakespeare and Marlowe', *SEL*, V, 1965, 247-68.

RABKIN, N. '*Venus and Adonis* and the myth of love', in McNEIR, W. F. and GREENFIELD, T. D. eds. *Pacific coast studies in Shakespeare*; Eugene, 1966, pp. 20-32.

## THE RAPE OF LUCRECE

*First edition:* First printed 1594. Facsimiles ed. F. J. Furnivall (1886); ed. S. Lee (1905); Elizabethan Club (1964).

*Modern editions:* Ed. G. Wyndham (1898); Arden, ed. C. K. Pooler (1911, 2nd ed., 1928); Yale, ed. A. Feuillerat (1927); New Temple, ed. M. R. Ridley (1935); New Variorum, ed. H. E. Rollins (1938); Penguin, ed. G. B. Harrison (1959); New Arden, ed. F. T. Prince (1960); ed. O. J. Campbell (1964); ed. E. Hubler (1964); New Cambridge, ed. J. C. Maxwell (1966).

### CRITICAL STUDIES

COLVIN, S. 'The sack of Troy in Shakespeare's *Lucrece* and in some 15th century drawings and tapestries', in GOLLANCZ, I. (ed.) *A Book of homage to Shakespeare*, 1916, pp. 88-99.

KUHL, E. P. 'Shakespeare's *Rape of Lucrece*', *PQ*, 1941, 352-60, and in *Renaissance studies in honor of Hardin Craig*; Stanford, 1941, pp. 160-8.

TOLBERT, J. M. 'The argument of Shakespeare's *Lucrece*; its sources and authorship', *UTSE*, XXIX, 1950, 77-90.

WALLEY, H. R. '*The Rape of Lucrece* and Shakespearean tragedy', *PMLA*, LXXVI, 1961, 480-7.

ALLEN, D. C. 'Some observations on the *Rape of Lucrece*', *ShS*, XV, 1962, 89-98.

MUIR, K. '*The Rape of Lucrece*', *Anglica*, V, 1964, 25-40.

STARNES, D. T. 'Geoffrey Fenton, Seneca and Shakespeare's *Lucrece*', *PQ*, XLIII, 1964, 280-3.

FRYE, R. M. 'Shakespeare's composition of *Lucrece*: new evidence', *ShQ*, XVI, 1965, 289-96.

## THE PASSIONATE PILGRIM

*First edition:* First printed 1599. Facsimile, ed. E. Dowden (1883); ed. S. Lee (1905); ed. J. Q. Adams (Washington, 1939); Cambridge (1964); Elizabethan Club (1964).

*Modern editions:* Arden, ed. C. K. Pooler (1911, 2nd ed., 1928); New Variorum, ed. H. E. Rollins (1938); New Arden, ed. F. T. Prince (1960); ed. O. J. Campbell (1964); ed. E. Hubler (1964); New Cambridge, ed. J. C. Maxwell (1966).

### CRITICAL STUDIES

KUHL, E. P. 'Shakespeare and the *Passionate Pilgrim*', *MLN*, XXXIV, 1919, 313-14.

## THE PHOENIX AND TURTLE

*First edition:* First printed 1601 with *Loves Martyr* by Robert Chester. Facsimile, Elizabethan Club (1964).

*Modern editions:* Ed. A. B. Grosart (1878); Yale, ed. A. Feuillerat (1927); Arden, ed. C. K. Pooler (1911, 2nd ed., 1928); New Temple, ed. M. R. Ridley (1935); New Variorum, ed. H. E. Rollins (1938); Penguin, ed. G. B. Harrison (1959); New Arden, ed. F. T. Prince (1960); ed. O. J. Campbell (1964); ed. F. Hubler (1964); New Cambridge, ed. J. C. Maxwell (1966).

### CRITICAL STUDIES

HALLIWELL-PHILLIPS, J. O. *Some account of Chester's 'Loves Martyr,'* 1865.

FAIRCHILD, A. H. R. '*The Phoenix and Turtle:* a critical and historical interpretation', *Englische Studien*, XXXIII, 1904, 337-84.

BROWN, C. *Poems by Sir John Salusbury, Robert Chester &c.*, *EETS*, 1913.

MURRY, J. Middleton. 'The nature of poetry', in *Discoveries*, 1924.

BONNARD, G. 'Shakespeare's contribution to R. Chester's *Loves Martyr: The Phoenix and the Turtle*', *ES*, XIX, 1937, 66-69.

SITWELL, O. 'The sole Arabian tree', *TLS*, 1941, 199, 206.

BENHAM, G. '*The Phoenix and the Turtle*', *TLS*, 1941, 352, 364.

BRADBROOK, M. '*The Phoenix and the Turtle*', *ShQ*, VI, 1955, 356-8.

CUNNINGHAM, J. V. ' "Essence" and *The Phoenix and the Turtle*', *ELH*, XIX, 1952, 265-76.

BATES, R. 'Shakespeare's *The Phoenix and the Turtle*', *ShQ*, VI, 1955, 19-30.

ONG, W. J. 'Metaphor and the twinned vision', *SeR*, LXIII, 1955, 193-201.

CUNNINGHAM, J. V. 'Idea as structure: *The Phoenix and the Turtle*', in *Tradition and poetic structure;* Denver, 1960, pp. 76-89.

RICHARDS, I. A. 'The sense of poetry: Shakespeare's *The Phoenix and the Turtle*', in MAY, R. (ed.) *Symbolism in religion and literature:* New York, 1960, pp. 203-14.

SELTZER, D. 'Their tragic scene', *ShQ*, XII, 1961, 91-101.

ELLRODT, R. 'An anatomy of *The Phoenix and the Turtle*', *ShS*, XV, 1962, 99-110.

BONAVENTURE, S. M. 'The phoenix renewed', *Forum*, V, 1964, 72-76.

COPLAND, M. 'The dead phoenix', *EC*, XV, 1965, 279-87.

MATCHETT, W. H. *The Phoenix and the Turtle;* The Hague, 1965.

EMPSON, W. '*The Phoenix and the Turtle*', *EC*, XVI, 1966, 147-53.


# SONNETS and *A LOVER'S COMPLAINT*

*First edition:* Shake-speares Sonnets. First printed 1609, with *A Lover's Complaint* appended. Facsimiles, ed. T. Tyler (1885); ed. S. Lee (1905); ed. A. T. B. (1925); ed. N. Douglas (1926); English replicas (New York, 1936); Elizabethan Club (1964).

*Modern editions:* Ed. E. Dowden (1881); ed. G. Wyndham (1898); ed. Samuel Butler (1899); ed. W. H. Hadow (1907); Variorum, ed. R. M. Alden (1916); Arden, ed. C. K. Pooler (1918); Yale, ed. E. B. Reed (1923); ed. T. G. Tucker (1924); New Temple, ed. M. R. Ridley (1935); ed. Tucker Brooke (1936); Penguin, ed. G. B. Harrison (1938); New Variorum, ed. H. E. Rollins (2 vols. 1944—*Lover's Complaint* included in 'Poems', 1938); Pelican, ed. D. Bush and A. Harbage (Baltimore, 1961); ed. M. Seymour-Smith (1963); ed. O. J. Campbell (1964); ed. W. G. Ingram and T. Redpath (1964); ed. A. L. Rowse (1964); New Cambridge, ed. J. Dover Wilson (1966—*Lover's Complaint* included in 'Poems', ed. J. C. Maxwell, 1966).


## CRITICAL STUDIES ETC.

BROWN, C. A. *Shakespeare's autobiographical poems*, 1838.

MASSEY, G. *The secret drama of Shakespeare's sonnets unfolded*, 1872.

WILDE, OSCAR. 'The portrait of Mr. W. H.', *Blackwood's Edinburgh Magazine*, CXLVI, July 1889, 1-21

—reprinted, with an introduction by Vyvyan Holland, 1958.

GODWIN, P. *A new study of the sonnets;* New York, 1900.

LEE, S. 'Ovid and Shakespeare's sonnets', *Quarterly Review*, CXX, 1909, 455-76, and in *Elizabethan and other essays*, 1929, pp. 116-39.

BATES, E. S. 'The sincerity of Shakespeare's sonnets', *MP*, VIII, 1910-11, 87-106.

MACKAIL, J. W. 'Shakespeare's sonnets', in *Lectures on poetry*, 1911, pp. 178-207.

MACKAIL, J. W. 'A Lover's Complaint', *ESEA*, III, 1912, 51-70.

ALDEN, R. M. 'The Quarto arrangement of Shakespeare's sonnets', in *G. L. Kittredge anniversary papers;* Boston, 1913, pp. 279-88.

SHAW, G. B. *The dark lady of the sonnets*, 1914.

ACHESON, A. *Shakespeare's sonnet story, 1592-8*, 1922.

REDIN, M. 'The friend in Shakespeare's sonnets', *Englische Studien*, LVI, 1922, 390-407.

LEE, S. *Life of Shakespeare*, 4th ed. 1925.

BECKWITH, E. 'On the chronology of Shakespeare's sonnets', *JEGP*, XXV, 1926, 227-42.

HARRISON, G. B. (ed.) *Willobie his Avisa*, 1926.

ROBERTSON, J. M. *The problems of the Shakespeare sonnets*, 1926.

BRAY, D. 'The art-form of the Elizabethan sonnet sequence and Shakespeare's sonnets', *ShJ*, LXIII, 1927, 159-82.

FORT, J. A. *A time-scheme for Shakespeare's sonnets*, 1929.

MURRY, J. Middleton. 'Problems of the Shakespeare sonnets', in *Countries of the mind*, Ser. 2. 1931, pp. 113-25.

WOOD, H. H. 'A 17th century MS of poems by Donne and others', *ESEA*, XVI, 1931, 179-90.

DOUGLAS, Lord Alfred. *The true history of Shakespeare's sonnets*, 1933.

FORT, J. A. 'The order and chronology of Shakespeare's sonnets', *RES*, IX, 1933, 19-23.

MATTINGLEY, G. 'The date of Shakespeare's sonnet CVII', *PMLA*, XLVIII, 1933, 705-21.

PEARSON, L. A. *Elizabethan love conventions;* Berkeley, 1933; reprinted 1964.

KNIGHTS, L. C. 'Revaluations, V: Shakespeare's sonnets', *ScR*, III, 1934, 133-60, and in *Explorations*, 1947, pp. 55-81.

NISBET, U. *The Onlie Begetter*, 1936.

ANGELL, P. K. 'Light on the "dark lady": a study of some Elizabethan libels', *PMLA*, LII, 1937, 652-74.

WELLS, H. W. 'A new preface to Shakespeare's sonnets', *SAB*, XII, 1937, 118-29.

YOUNG, H. M. *The sonnets of Shakespeare: a psycho-sexual analysis;* Columbia, 1937.

BRAY, D. *Shakespeare's sonnet sequence,* 1938.

CHAPMAN, J. A. 'Marching song', *ESEA,* XXVIII, 1942, 13-21.

ANSPACHER, L. K. *Shakespeare as poet and lover and the enigma of the sonnets;* New York, 1944.

CARTER, A. H. 'The punctuation of Shakespeare's Sonnets of 1609', in MACMANAWAY, J. G. (ed.) *Joseph Quincy Adams Memorial studies,* 1948, pp. 409-28.

GRAY, H. D. 'Shakespeare's rival poet', *JEGP,* XLVII, 1948, 365-73.

HOTSON, L. *Shakespeare's sonnets dated and other essays,* 1949.

GOLDSMITH, U. K. 'Words out of a hat? Alliteration and assonance in Shakespeare's sonnets', *JEGP,* XLIX, 1950, 33-48.

EMPSON, W. *Some versions of Pastoral,* 1950.

HARBAGE, A. 'Dating Shakespeare's sonnets', *ShQ,* I, 1950, 57-63.

BATESON, F. W. 'Elementary my dear Hotson', *EC,* I, 1951, 81-88.

HOTSON, L. 'More light on Shakespeare's sonnets', *ShQ,* II, 1951, 111-18.

NOSWORTHY, J. M. 'All too short a date: internal evidence in Shakespeare's sonnets', *EC,* II, 1952, 311-24.

NOWOTTNY, W. M. T. 'Formal elements in Shakespeare's sonnets: sonnets I-VI, *EC,* II, 1952, 76-84.

HUBLER, E. *The sense of Shakespeare's sonnets;* Princeton, 1952.

CRUTTWELL, P. 'A reading of the sonnets', *Hudson Review,* V, 1953, 554-70.

HUNTER, G. K. 'The dramatic technique of Shakespeare's sonnets', *EC,* III, 1953, 152-64.

STONE, W. B. 'Shakespeare and the "sad augurs" ', *JEGP,* LII, 1953, 457-79.

MASSON, D. I. 'Free phonetic patterns in Shakespeare's sonnets', *Neophilologus,* XXXVIII, 1954, 277-89.

LEVER, J. W. *The Elizabethan love sonnet,* 1956; 2nd ed. 1966.

BROWN, I. *Dark ladies,* 1957.

BERRY, F. ' "Thou" and "You" in Shakespeare's sonnets', *EC,* VIII, 1958, 138-46.

TAYLOR, D. 'The Earl of Pembroke and the youth of Shakespeare's sonnets', *SP,* LVI, 1959, 26-54.

GERARD, A. S. 'The stone as lily: a discussion of Shakespeare's sonnet XCIV.', *ShJ,* XCVI, 1960, 155-60.

ROSTENBERG, L. 'Thomas Thorpe, publisher of Shakespeare's sonnets', *PBSA*, LIV, 1960, 16-37.

SCHAAR, C. *An Elizabethan sonnet problem;* Lund, 1960.

STIRLING, B. 'A Shakespeare sonnet group'. *PMLA*, LXXV, 1960, 340-9.

LEISHMAN, J. B. *Themes and variations in Shakespeare sonnets*, 1961; 2nd ed. 1963, reprinted 1967.

GRUNDY, J. 'Shakespeare's sonnets and the Elizabethan sonneteers', *ShS*, XV, 1962, 41-49.

HUBLER, E. (and others). *The riddle of Shakespeare's sonnets: the text with interpretive essays;* New York, 1962.

NEJGEBAUER, A. 'The sonnets', *ShS*, XV, 1962, 10-18.

SCHAAR, C. *Elizabethan sonnet themes and the dating of Shakespeare's Sonnets';* Lund, 1962.

BARBER, C. L. 'Shakespeare in his Sonnets', *Massachusetts Review*, Aug., 1960, 648-72.

SOUTHAM, B. C. 'Shakespeare's Christian Sonnet': Number 146', *ShQ*, XI, 1960, 67-71.

BLACKMUR, R. P. 'A poetics of infatuation', *Kenyon Review*, XXIII, 1961, 647-70.

GERARD, A. 'Iconic organization in Shakespeare's Sonnet 146', *ES*, XLII, 1961, 157-9.

GITTINGS, R. *Shakespeare's rival*, 1961.

GREEN, A. W. 'Significant words in Shakespeare's sonnets', *University of Mississippi Studies in English*, III, 1962, 95-113.

MAHOOD, M. M. 'Love's confined doom', *ShS*, XV, 1962, 50-61.

NEARING, Homer, Jr. 'Shakespeare as a nondramatic poet: sonnet 29', *ShQ*, XIII, 1962, 15-20.

EVANS, E. C. 'Shakespeare's Sonnet 97', *RES*, n.s. XVI, 1963, 379-80.

KAULA, David. ' "In war with time": temporal perspectives in Shakespeare's sonnets', *SEL*, III, 1963, 45-57.

KNIGHT, G. Wilson. 'Shakespeare' sonnets', *TLS*, 1963, 1072.

LANDRY, H. 'Malone as editor of Shakespeare's sonnets', *Bulletin of the New York Public Library*, LXVII, 1963, 435-42.

LANDRY, H. *Interpretations in Shakespeare's sonnets';* Berkeley, 1963.

NOSWORTHY, J. M. 'Shakespeare and Mr. W. H.', *Library*, XVIII, 1963, 294-8.

PIRKHOFER, A. M. ' "A pleasing pretty pricket": on the use of alliteration in Shakespeare's sonnets', *ShQ*, XIV, 1963, 3-14.

STIRLING, B. 'More Shakespeare sonnet groups', in HOSLEY, R. ed. *Essays on Shakespeare and Elizabethan drama*, 1963, pp. 115-35.

WILSON, J. D. *An introduction to the sonnets of Shakespeare for the use of historians and others;* Cambridge, 1963.

AUDEN, W. H. 'Shakespeare's sonnets', *The Listener*, LXXII, 1964, 7-9, 45-47.

DOEBLER, J. 'Submerged element in Sonnet 116', *ShQ*, 1964, 109-10.

GRIFFIN, R. J. ' "These contraries such unity do hold": patterned imagery in Shakespeare's narrative poems', *SEL*, IV, 1964, 43-55.

HOTSON, Leslie, *Mr. W. H.*, 1964.

KNIGHT, G. Wilson. 'New light on Shakespeare's sonnets', *The Listener*, LXXI, 1964, 715-17.

KRIEGER, N. *A window to criticism: Shakespeare's sonnets and modern poetics;* Princeton, 1964.

LEVIN, R. 'Shakespeare's sonnet 97', *RES*, XV, 1964, 408-9.

MUIR, K. *'A Lover's Complaint* a reconsideration', in BLOOM, E. A. ed. *Shakespeare, 1564-1964;* Providence, 1964, pp. 154-66.

PURDUM, R. 'Shakespeare's sonnet 128', *JEGP*, LXIII, 1964, 235-9.

SCHAAR, C. 'Conventional and unconventional in the descriptions of scenery in Shakespeare's sonnets', *ES*, XLV, 1964, 142-9.

SILVERSTEIN, N. 'Shakespeare's sonnets in perspective', *Forum*, V, 1964, 67-71.

STIRLING, B. 'Sonnets 109-26', *Centennial Review of Arts & Science (Michigan)*, VIII, 1964, 109-20.

STIRLING, B. 'Sonnets 127-134', in BLOOM, E. A. ed. *Shakespeare 1564-1964;* Providence, 1964, pp. 134-53.

WILLEN, G. and REED, V. B. eds. *A casebook on Shakespeare's sonnets;* New York, 1964.

LEVIN, R. 'Sonnet 129 as a dramatic poem', *ShQ*, XVI, 1965, 175-81.

REICHERT, J. F. 'Sonnet 20 and Erasmus's epistle to persuade a young gentleman to marriage', *ShQ*, 16, 1965, 238-40.

TATE, A. 'The unilateral imagination', *Southern Review*, N.S. I, 1965, 530-42.

TOLIVER, H. E. 'Shakespeare and the abyss of time', *JEGP*, LXIV, 1965, 234-54.

LEISI, E. 'A possible emendation of Shakespeare's sonnet 146', *ES*, XLVII, 1966, 271-85.

THOMSON, P. 'The date clue in Shakespeare's sonnet 98', *Neophilologus*, L, 1966, 262-7.

# THE WORKS OF WILLIAM SHAKESPEARE

## GRAMOPHONE RECORDS

The works of Shakespeare have been recorded, complete and uncut in the text of the New Shakespeare edited by John Dover Wilson, by leading professional players with the Marlowe Dramatic Society of Cambridge University. The series is directed by George Rylands, Fellow of King's College, Cambridge, and the musical director is Thurston Dart. Among those taking part are:

| | |
|---|---|
| MAX ADRIAN | MILES MALLESON |
| PEGGY ASHCROFT | PETER PEARS |
| JILL BALCON | PRUNELLA SCALES |
| TONY CHURCH | MARGARETTA SCOTT |
| WILLIAM DEVLIN | WILLIAM SQUIRE |
| JOHN GIELGUD | DOROTHY TUTIN |
| DEREK GODFREY | GARY WATSON |
| MICHAEL HORDERN | IRENE WORTH |
| RICHARD JOHNSON | PATRICK WYMARK |

The recordings, in mono and stereo, made under the auspices of the British Council, are issued by Argo, 113 Fulham Road, London, S.W.3.

| | | | | | |
|---|---|---|---|---|---|
| ALL'S WELL THAT | RG | 354–6 | HENRY V | RG | 261–4 |
| ENDS WELL | ZRG | 5354–6 | | ZRG | 5261–4 |
| AS YOU LIKE IT | RG | 125–7 | HENRY VI Part 1 | RG | 386–8 |
| ANTONY AND | RG | 307–10 | | ZRG | 5386–8 |
| CLEOPATRA | ZRG | 5307–10 | HENRY VI Part 2 | RG | 389–92 |
| THE COMEDY OF | RG | 311–2 | | ZRG | 5389–92 |
| ERRORS | ZRG | 5311–2 | HENRY VI Part 3 | RG | 393–6 |
| CORIOLANUS | RG | 135–8 | | ZRG | 5393–6 |
| CYMBELINE | RG | 265–8 | HENRY VIII | RG | 303–6 |
| | ZRG | 5265–8 | | ZRG | 5303–6 |
| HAMLET | RG | 256–60 | JULIUS CAESAR | RG | 132–4 |
| | ZRG | 5256–60 | | | |
| HENRY IV Part 1 | RG | 208–11 | KING JOHN | RG | 168–71 |
| | ZRG | 5208–11 | | ZRG | 5168–71 |
| HENRY IV Part 2 | RG | 212–5 | KING LEAR | RG | 280–3 |
| | ZRG | 5212–5 | | ZRG | 5280–3 |

| | | | | | | |
|---|---|---|---|---|---|---|
| LOVE'S LABOUR'S | RG | 313–5 | ROMEO AND JULIET | RG | 200–3 |
| LOST | ZRG | 5313–5 | | ZRG | 5200–3 |
| MACBETH | RG | 175–7 | THE SONNETS | RG | 142–4 |
| | ZRG | 5175–7 | THE TAMING OF | RG | 348–50 |
| MEASURE FOR | RG | 164–7 | THE SHREW | ZRG | 5348–50 |
| MEASURE | ZRG | 5164–7 | THE TEMPEST | RG | 216–8 |
| THE MERCHANT OF | RG | 160–3 | | ZRG | 5216–8 |
| VENICE | ZRG | 5160–3 | TIMON OF ATHENS | RG | 253–5 |
| THE MERRY WIVES | RG | 351–3 | | ZRG | 5253–5 |
| OF WINDSOR | ZRG | 5351–3 | TITUS ANDRONICUS | RG | 357–9 |
| A MIDSUMMER | RG | 250–2 | | ZRG | 5357–9 |
| NIGHT'S DREAM | ZRG | 5250–2 | TROILUS AND | | |
| MUCH ADO ABOUT | RG | 300–2 | CRESSIDA | RG | 128–31 |
| NOTHING | ZRG | 5300–2 | TWELFTH NIGHT | RG | 284–6 |
| OTHELLO | RG | 121–4 | | ZRG | 5284–6 |
| PERICLES, PRINCE | RG | 411–13 | THE TWO GENTLEMEN | RG | 172–4 |
| OF TYRE | ZRG | 5411–13 | OF VERONA | ZRG | 5172–4 |
| THE RAPE OF | | | VENUS AND ADONIS | RG | 336–7 |
| LUCRECE | RG | 334–5 | THE WINTER'S TALE | RG | 204–7 |
| RICHARD II | RG | 139–41 | | ZRG | 5204–7 |
| RICHARD III | RG | 407–10 | | | |
| | ZRG | 5407–10 | *ZRG denotes stereophonic record.* | | |